To the Caregiver,

This story is about what makes our friends different. It explains 16 different disabilities/differences to spread awareness about why people have different needs!

This book uses muted tones and simple illustrations to keep the focus on the meaning of the words!

I hope you'll use this story to educate children about disabilities and diversity, to pave a better future for all!

All my friends are different, two people the same are rare,

let's celebrate our differences to show others that we care.

We'll split our learning into two to help you understand,

Visible **Invisible**

we'll learn about different people and why they might need a helping hand!

Visible differences are something you can see,

let's read all about it, come with me.

Gabe wears glasses on his face to help his eyes see clearer,

he can't see birds in the tree but can see them when they're nearer!

Blake is blind, her eyes only see fog,

she carries a cane and has a Guide Dog!

Hakeem has a hearing aid, he's deaf in one ear,

Waving our hand is how we sign "hello!"

He uses Sign Language because he cannot hear!

Flora has a feeding tube, she finds eating tough,

the tube takes food in through her nose to give her the right stuff!

William has a wheelchair, because his legs are numb,

he controls where he goes by moving his thumb!

Evie has braces she wears for support,

she has EDS and struggles with sport!

Fletcher has a frame, to help him walk is it's goal,

it helps him move faster, look he's on a roll!

Dahlia has Down's Syndrome, she looks different than me,

inviting her to play makes her face light up with glee!

An invisible difference is hidden from sight,

Invisible

do you know some already?
I think you might!

Alex has Autism, it changes his brain,

he likes things lined up, he likes things the same!

Avery has ADHD, her mind is always busy,

she has much bigger senses that can make her brain feel fizzy!

Ali has Auditory Processing Disorder, everything's louder in his brain,

he takes more time to answer your questions, some sounds can cause him pain!

Sadie has Sensory Processing Disorder, she's similar to her friend Ali,

for Sadie it's every sense that feels big, from taste to touch, smell to see!

Daniel has Dyslexia, he struggles to read books,

his brain can't understand the words no matter how hard he looks!

Darcy has Dyspraxia, she's as clumsy as can be,

she struggles to say words clearly, but she tries her best you see!

Noah is Non-Verbal, he has a special way

of sharing his ideas with us, he still has lots to say!

Dale has Developmental Delay, he's a bit behind his friends,

he'll get there in his own time, we're all different in the end!

All my friends are different, it's very clear to see,

we celebrate our differences as one big family!

No two are the same and we like it this way,

you were born to change the world, whatever comes your way!

Look past what makes us different, love with all your heart,

when it comes to kindness there's no better time to start!

Printed in Great Britain
by Amazon

CHEZ BECCY
HOMEWARE · ACCESSORIES

BAKING DEMONSTRATION & AFTERNOON TEA

Join Beccy for a delightful informal afternoon in her kitchen drinking tea whilst Beccy lets you into her baking secrets!

Scan the QR code for more information

www.chezbeccy.com

CHEZ BECCY

HOMEWARE · ACCESSORIES

Wrap your kitchen in the warmth of British craftsmanship!

Sign up to our mailing list to get your 15% off your first order.

Discover our collection of kitchen textiles, proudly made in Britain.

From charming tea towels to stylish aprons & reliable oven gloves, each piece is a testament to our heritage.

www.chezbeccy.com